Starlings' Sweet Symphonies

Megan O'Brien

BookLeaf Publishing

Presentation by *BookLeaf Publishing*

Web: www.bookleafpub.com

E-mail: info@bookleafpub.com

ISBN: 9789357615587

First edition 2022

For Mom and Dad

ACKNOWLEDGEMENT

Thank you to family, friends and teachers who encouraged my writing, especially Mr. Cauchi.

PREFACE

This is a collection of poetry written over almost 20 years.

Flowers

Flowers come in many colors,
sizes and shapes too,
Carnations can be pink or yellow,
violets come in purple or blue.
Roses grow on long thin stems,
lined with prickly thorns,
And other flowers like daffodils,
 are oddly shaped like horns.

The Beach

I like to walk along the beach,
and look at the birds that are out of reach,
the wave comes in and then it crashes,
against the boulders it fiercely smashes,
smoothing glass and washing up rocks,
while seagulls fly away in flocks.
The sandy beach, it is still wet,
while the yellow sun begins to set.

Nature Set

The sun is rising,
up out of the wheat valleys,
as it drifts toward sea.

The cloud flows by me,
it is moving very slowly,
almost not at all.

The Coming of New

When a new baby comes,
the world is new,
and the day dawns magnificently
as the sun shines for the first time.
As a new page is turned and a new story written,
the roses excrete pure fragrance
while a rainbow is formed in perfect symmetry
with the fresh horizon,
and the sky reaches from never to eternity,
when a new baby comes.

The Butterfly

5

The butterfly dances,
among the stale breeze,
then falls softly, unheard.

Birth of Stars

Walking on the grainy beads,
whispering winds tickling our backs,
golden rays warm upon our faces,
waves reaching fiercely from a far,
birds sailing along the shore,
the sun dies as stars are born,
the winds begin to howl piercingly,
the sands eat our feet,
the waves encroach, threatening our security,
We hide behind a stable boulder, hoping the
storm will pass.

Untitled

Born into skies of blue and fields of green,
my dewed petals dancing in the warm noon
wind,
my young branches brushing the new soil,
my small feathered extensions flapping as I
soared high over trees with heads of amber-gold
and sugary sweet greens,
encased in a world of starlings' sweet
symphonies,
I knew nothing of the real world.

Now the wind is chilling,
forcing my petals from me one by one,
my bare, leafless branches left exposed,
are reaching for that intangeable brown warmth,
my blue skies have been torn from my grasp,
and above are ever darkening clouds of despair,
shading me from the red-golden beams that are
struggling to break through,
the icy pelts stinging me,
with cold whispers closing in on me,
the starlings' sweet melodies now drowned by
their harsh screams, my screams.
I know nothing of this cruel, real world.

The Night

Dark reaching arms that grab in the night,
singing whispers to any who will listen,
beckoning the weak,
to join those who have lost their souls,
and buried them deep in the caverns of insanity,
those who laugh together,
but know no real joy,
those who cry,
but know no true sadness,
the ones who scream from false pain,
hidden behind dancing shadows that fall when
the music stops,
they fly over hopeless souls,
searching in the night.

Time

Time grays the sands,
with inevitable duty,
and dries the seas with reluctant pleasure,
it salts the trees by moonlight,
and turns the pages of space with a wrinkled
hand.
Tarnishing blades of grass,
it strikes the desert in the night,
it makes a beginning at the end,
and all that's left is Earth and sky.

A Night Set Piece

I sit on a severed tree,
in the light of the big round moon,
the boy holding up the oak calls to me,
the teacher yells, "over 1-2, hop back, hop back",
as the wind whistles through my hair,
the jig music plays, "dee da lee dee, dee da lee dee"
as I realize, only now am I truly happy.

I Will

I will the sky to open wide,
and shower down on me,
to let me taste her bitter-sweet wine,
and set my sad soul free,
to cleanse my hands of ill deeds done,
and erase the stabbing memories from my mind,
to lift my heart to drier land,
where it can dance happily in the sublime.
I will the sun to burn my face,
and leave no traces of my past,
to scar the skin that scarred so many,
and left them twitching among the glass.
I will the wind to bite my bones,
so I shall know the wrong from right,
and take what has been coming to me,
rather than running in the night.
I beg the sea to lift its arms,
and carry me away,
I wish to taste his salty love,
I haven't the strength to be saved today.

For Dad

It was long ago, in days of old,
I made you a knight, and you were brave and
bold,
When myths and legends true were told,
and laying on gray stones was cold.

We dug for treasures deep, of gold,
and with our swords of steel to hold
we made armies of the thousands fold
and sleeping on black stones was cold.

We slayed dragons who breathed fire,
we were fierce and would never tire,
We hiked up hills and through the mire,
and bowed at the knees of kings and sires,

But there is no time left to warm,
for the buzzards have begun to swarm
and now our resting stones are warm.

True Baptism

True baptism comes when I forget to remember
the past,
and run outside as the milk-like flakes begin to
fall on my fingers,
the cold powder stars so sweet,
they burn my soul,
I stand with arms reached high
and catch the little flecks of eternity falling on
my tongue.
I lie on the whitening ground and let the frozen
holy water shower me.
I close my eyes and cleanse my mind as I feel
each piece of heaven slip between my toes.
When I am free to laugh with the wind,
and live now for only this moment,
because now is beautiful,
and in my inner church
I receive true baptism.

There is the Moon

There is the moon,
when there is no one else,
and all the rest have run,
There is the moon,
when I'm all alone
and the maddening day is done.
There is a moon that calls to me
and whispers in my ear,
Night after night, she rescues me
when I am drowning in my fear.
She reigns from way above my world
and keeps a watchful eye,
She never lets me fall too far,
my keeper in the sky.
There is a moon that lives in me,
buried deep within,
and on the day you come for me
her moonlight shower will begin.

When Evil Dies

Moonlit dance
promise prance
euphoric trance
there's but one chance.
Twisted dreams
acid teems
shine and gleam
what do they mean?
Humble cry
evil's alive
The reasons why?
I had to try.
Now I fly
as evil dies
no more lies
protected pride.

Colored Leaves (for Buddy)

Your smiling eyes,
your warm embrace,
your tender touch,
your style and grace.

The way you'd always take the time
to hear what I had to say,
The way your few kind words
could brighten up my day.

And how you always thought to give,
before you'd think to take,
and how you always remembered all the friends
that you would make.

In the way that you would say
with the stroke of your hand,
that you really care and truly understand.

Your devotion to your family
and the love you were always showing,
brought us happy days
and gave us the strength to keep on going,
and now that you have left us,
and we are all alone

we must hold on to all the many good times we
have known.

As the trees begin to die,
and the many colored leaves run by,
you watch us from way up high
and keep a close and watchful eye.
As we watch the night stars light the sky,
we grab hands but do not cry,
for now we must say goodbye.
We know your love can never die.

Haiku in Three Seasons

Golden-amber leaves
fall softly upon the ground,
rustling at my feet.

Gleaming rays shine down,
through clouds far above my head,
calling me to rise.

Crystalline flakes fall,
upon the leafless branches,
keep them safe and warm.

These Trees

Sweet wet breeze
hear it rustle through the trees
Taste the chilly dew of morning,
as it frolics in the leaves.

Crisp, cool air
I watch it flying through your hair
And the shadows that the trees throw down,
seem to simply point and stare.

In days of old, when we were young,
and being a child meant having fun,
We'd run and hide among these trees
and wait until the day was done.

And now that we are grown, you see
and our lives aren't as we thought they'd be,
We long for those sweet, fresh days of youth,
and the safety in the arms of these trees.

Drops of Me

Rain
Small wet drops
falling on my tongue,
light and soft and sweet.

Rain
Big strong drops
crashing at my feet.

Sea
Crystal blue glass
warm inviting smile.

Sea
Thrashing salty arms
enticing every child.

River
Calm, cool, steady

River
Fierce, wild, ready

Rain
Drops of me keep falling.

Tell Me

Tell me where it hurts now, baby
and I'll wash it all away,
all the pain and tears of all the years,
It's all in your eyes today.

Tell me where it hurts now, baby
and I'll make it disappear,
all the wrongs she did and what she couldn't give
I feel it in your arms when you hold me near.

Tell me where it hurts now, baby
and we'll kiss them right goodbye,
all the mistakes,
what made your poor heart break,
and you'll never hear another lie.

Tell me where it hurts now, baby
and I'll touch you magically,
and deep inside
You'll feel a cry
as I set your wounded soul free.

Remember

It was on that rain filled night,
when I could barely see the moon,
when the clouds were near invisible,
and I heard no night birds croon.

When the sky was gray as smoke,
and the rain fell soft and slow,
as I looked out from my window,
I began to realize what you already know,
that times change and things change and people,
they change too,
that what we had is in the past
and you're consumed with something new.
That this is life, constantly moving,
changing every day,
and there's nothing to undo it,
and no words to take it away,

Just as the sun will rise and set
our lives will grow apart,
and the end of our time together
is as important as the start,

But know that I am always here,
no matter where you go or what you do,

I will stay right here with a warm embrace and
wait
because I am a part of you.

So as sure as the rain will fall again,
and the summer sky will be blue,
when you don't call or visit, my friend,
I won't forget, I will always remember
you.